Learn to Be a Confident Public Speaker!

Discover new ways to be a memorable speaker in 15 steps

In this informative Itty Bitty book, Lisa Haisha teaches you how to navigate through the vast industry of Keynote Speaking. Included are tips and guidelines that will not only help you speak to live audiences, but give you the confidence and skills to communicate with anyone.

Use these helpful tools and tips to help you grow and develop your public speaking skills.

For example:

- Learning important speaking components, from writing the speech to delivery
- Finding your unique voice
- Learning to find your niche and book speaking gigs

Pick up a copy of this important book today. Remove your fears and experience the art of public speaking and powerful communication in all areas of your life.

Your Amazing Itty Bitty® How to Become a Keynote Speaker

15 Crucial Steps to Becoming a Captivating and Memorable Speaker in Your Field

Lisa Haisha, M.A.

Published by Itty Bitty® Publishing
A subsidiary of S & P Productions, Inc.

Copyright © 2019 Lisa Haisha

All rights reserved. No part of this book may be reproduced or transmitted in any form or by any means, electronic or mechanical, including photocopying, recording or by any information storage and retrieval system, without written permission of the publisher, except for inclusion of brief quotations in a review.

Printed in the United States of America

Itty Bitty Publishing
311 Main Street, Suite D
El Segundo, CA 90245
(310) 640-8885

ISBN: 978-1-950326-05-1

This book is dedicated to all the future speakers and storytellers who want to make a positive difference in the world.

Stop by our Itty Bitty® website to find to interesting blog entries regarding public speaking.

www.IttyBittyPublishing.com

Or visit Lisa Haisha at

www.LisaHaisha.com

Table of Contents

- Step 1. How to Speak Effectively
- Step 2. How to Make a Living as a Keynote Speaker
- Step 3. How to Get a Paid Speaking Gig
- Step 4. How to Speak for Free
- Step 5. What if I Can Speak but Can't Write?
- Step 6. How to Create Interesting Content
- Step 7. Most Engaging Presenter Behaviors
- Step 8. How to Deliver a Speech
- Step 9. Find a Mentor
- Step 10. Join a Speaker Association
- Step 11. Find Your Unique Voice
- Step 12. Take Off Your Impostor Mask
- Step 13. Create Evergreen Products
- Step 14. Establish Yourself as an Expert in Your Niche
- Step 15. Preparation is Everything

Introduction

Do you have extensive knowledge on a particular subject or in a particular niche that you want to share with others? Do you want to get paid to travel the world speaking at various events like; seminars, conferences, and conventions about your niche? Do you have an interest in becoming a keynote speaker, but you aren't sure how to get started? If you answered yes to any of these questions, then you will want to read this book about how to become a keynote speaker.

As a keynote speaker, you can make a huge impact on the lives of many people, as well as your own. One of the biggest benefits of being a speaker is you get to travel and connect with people all over the country and sometimes the world. You could go from speaking in corporate America to cruise ships. As a speaker you'll have the opportunity to speak to niche groups to inspire, motivate and create change.

Most importantly, you will get to do what you love doing. This book will be the first step on this amazing journey. It will teach you the skills you need to know to not only be a keynote speaker, but to be a successful and *great* keynote speaker.

Step 1
How to Speak Effectively

To be an effective keynote speaker, you need to grab your audience's attention and keep them engaged in what you're saying. You can do this through the use of storytelling, humor, and a call to action. In this chapter, we will go over the different methods and how to use them.

1. Storytelling
2. Humor
3. Call to Action

Effective Speaking Components

- **Storytelling:** Tell your audience a story that they can relate to and that will grip them with emotion.
- **Humor:** Including humor into your speech will help you engage your audience. You want your speech to be memorable, but you want them to remember it because you really spoke to them and pulled them in.
- **Call to Action.** This is where you ask your audience to take the next step. You tell them what they need to do when they leave.

For Example:

- Buy a product
- Read a particular article
- Visit a website
- Sign a petition
- Call legislators
- Support your cause

Don't make the mistake of sounding like you're begging your audience to do anything for *you.* All you need to do is point out the ways in which this call to action will benefit *them.*

Step 2
How to Make a Living as a Keynote Speaker

Becoming a keynote speaker can be the start of a very fulfilling and lucrative career. What better way is there to make a living than traveling around the country to talk to people about the topics you're passionate about? In this chapter you will learn what methods you can use to start making a living as a keynote speaker.

1. Speaking at Events
2. Training Courses
3. Selling Products
4. Coaching and Writing

Making a Living as a Speaker Components

- **Speaking at Events.** You can speak at colleges, universities, seminars, workshops, cruise ships, charity events, conventions and many more.
- **Training Courses.** Many keynote speakers develop their own training courses or they partner with people such as digital marketers or other keynote speakers to create training courses together. These training courses can be taught in person or can be recorded and sold in video format.
- **Selling Products.** You can create different types of products relevant to your niche and then sell these products online or at speaking events. Even if you speak for free at an event, you can still make money from that event by selling your products.
- **Coaching and Writing.** Once you have some experience under your belt, you can start coaching and also write speeches for other speakers. What you would earn from this is completely up to how much you charge for your services.

Step 3
How to Get Paid Speaking Gigs

As a keynote speaker with little experience, you are going to have to work a lot harder to land a paid speaking gig than someone who's been at it for several years. However, that does not mean it is impossible.

1. Decide Where You Want to Speak
2. Connect With People
3. Search Google

Paid Speaking Gigs

- **Decide Where You Want to Speak**. As a beginner, it's better to start small and work your way up. Be specific.
  - Next, create a pitch and send it to the appropriate person at each venue you hope to speak at. Don't be discouraged if you don't get a response or if the response you do get is a rejection. Even seasoned pros still get rejections once in a while. Keep trying and eventually you'll get a yes.
- **Connect With People.** Use social media to your advantage. Find other speakers in your field and connect with them. If you can build a relationship with other speakers, you could exchange advice and collaborate together. You may even get lucky enough to have them recommend you.
- **Search Google**. Use Google to search for events like conferences, seminars, and conventions in your field. Remember, if you're a beginner, it is best to start with free venues and a place like toastmasters, (non-profit speaking club) to practice weekly.

Step 4
How to Speak for Free

If you want to get your foot in the door and get your name out there as a keynote speaker, one of the best ways to do that is to speak for free at venues and events. If you want to make a living doing keynote speaking, you won't want to do free gigs all the time, but when you're just starting out, you can use those free gigs to your advantage. Here is a list of places where you can speak for free.

Examples:

1. Cruise Ships
2. Breakfast Meetings
3. Organizations in Your Niche
4. Conferences
5. Local Organizations and Clubs

Places To Speak For Free

- **Cruise Ships**. Cruise ships are always looking for speakers, and while you usually won't get paid to speak, you do get a free cruise out of it! This is also a great opportunity to build your email list, and sell your branded extended learning products such as: books, CD'S and online programs.
- **Breakfast Meetings**. Law firms, real estate agencies, women's groups and other meet ups often hold breakfast meetings and will invite people to speak, usually for free, but you may get lucky and land a paying gig.
- **Volunteer at Organizations**. If there is a particular organization that falls in your niche that you'd love to have the opportunity to speak, contact them and volunteer to speak at their next event.
- **Submit Ideas to Conferences**. If there is a conference coming up in the near future that you're interested in speaking at, send them your ideas.
- **Local Organizations and Clubs**. No matter where you live, there are organizations and community clubs where you could speak to an audience about your niche.

Step 5
What if I Can Speak but Can't Write?

You want to be a keynote speaker, but you don't think you can write, so now what? Even if you think you can't write, you can *learn* to write. Your other option would be to hire someone to write your speech for you. This chapter will discuss both options, so you can choose which way would work better for you.

1. Learn to Write
2. Hire a Speech Writer

Learn to Write
- Start by making an outline listing the main points you want to make in your speech.
- Study well-known speeches that keynote speakers have given, so you can see how they have outlined their speeches.
- Take a speech-writing course.

Hire a Speech Writer

- You will need to supply the writer with an outline of the points you want to make, and relevant personal stories that will enhance your speech.
- They will establish your speaking style; speaking pace, tone, etc. that will aide them in writing a speech that will sound authentic to you.
- Do your research. Hire a writer who has experience writing strong and successful speeches.
- The best choice is not only a good speech writer, but the one with real life experience within the topic.

Step 6
How to Create Interesting Content

If you want to be a successful keynote speaker and build a brand for yourself then you need to have interesting content so that you can build a following and continue to keep that following engaged.

There are many ways you can go about creating interesting content not only for your keynote speeches, but also for your website, blog, newsletters, podcasts, webinars, and any other types of media you use.

1. Find Out What Your Followers Want to Know
2. Have Original Content
3. Use Infographics
4. Include a Story
5. Use Pictures

Content

- **Find out what your followers want to know.** When you are creating content, think about the kinds of questions they might ask about your topic or niche, and then build your content around answering those questions.
- **Have original content.** Even if it's the same information that can be found on other websites or books, if you come at it from a different angle, it will seem like entirely new information to your audience.
- **Use infographics.** Create an infographic for your topic so all the information you want your audience to know will be in one place.
- **Include a personal story.** Think of a relatable story that pertains to your topic and then weave it into your speech or website content. You will engage your audience while also building a relationship.
- **Use pictures.** When writing a piece pictures help set the mood and tone of the content. Pictures grab the attention of the reader and helps provide a deeper understanding of all written media, (blogs, websites, articles, branded brochures, etc.).

Step 7
Most Engaging Presenter Behaviors

To be a successful keynote speaker, you have to learn the best ways to engage your audience throughout your entire presentation. If you have studied other keynote speakers' methods, then you have probably caught on to some of the more common engaging presenter behaviors. If you haven't, you should—that is one of the best ways to grow as a speaker. You will learn about several of them in this chapter, so you can implement them into your next keynote speech.

1. Keep Your Presentations Short
2. Use Pauses and Silence Effectively
3. Use Hand Gestures and Movement
4. Insert Humor
5. Tell Stories

How To Be Interesting

- **Keep Your Presentation Short.** Shorter presentations allow you to keep your audience's attention. They'll be satisfied at the amount of information they received in a short amount of time.
- **Use Pauses and Silences Effectively.** Pauses and silences usually occur after the speaker has said something that they want their audience to really think about. If used appropriately, pauses and silences at the right times, can turn an ordinary speech into an extraordinary speech.
- **Use Hand Gestures and Movement.** Moving around benefits you by helping to take away some of the anxiety you might be feeling. It also keeps the audience engaged.
- **Insert Humor.** Humor helps to make your speech more entertaining and less like an info dump.
- **Tell Stories.** The best place to include a story in your speech is within the first 10 minutes.

Step 8
How to Deliver a Speech

Is there anything more nerve-racking than getting up on a stage in front of a huge crowd of people to give a speech? Some would probably say that it's a piece of cake, but most keynote speakers feel quite a bit of anxiety when they're up on that stage. Those nerves can cause you to lose your train of thought, or say the wrong thing, or make any one of a number of other mistakes. The best way to knock some of those nerves to the ground is to go up on that stage confident in your ability to deliver a great speech. To do that, you need to be prepared. Here are a few tips to help you deliver a speech with the utmost confidence.

1. Have a Goal
2. Memorize the Speech
3. Transition Naturally
4. Speak Clearly
5. Use Infographics
6. Be Yourself

Delivery

- **Have a Goal.** What do you want the audience to be thinking about? What purpose are you trying to convey to them? How do you want them to feel? What actions do you want them to take?
- **Memorize the Speech.** You will be able to engage your audience better by maintaining eye contact. Speaking from memory instead of a piece of paper will also make your speech sound more authentic.
- **Transition Naturally.** You want the transition between two points to sound natural. Think about what words you will use to get from point A to point B.
- **Speak Clearly.** Record yourself reciting your speech and listen to the playback. Can you understand you?
- **Use Infographics.** Infographics will allow you to display additional details that you don't need to include in your actual speech.
- **Be Yourself.** Act natural. You don't have to be perfect. Your audience will appreciate you and what you're saying a lot more if they can see you as you are.

Step 9
Find a Mentor Who Speaks Or Hire a Speaking Coach

Many keynote speakers perfected their public speaking skills with the help of a mentor or a speaking coach. This is not something that you have to do to be a professional speaker. However, it is a step that you may consider when first starting out to help you build your confidence and sharpen your skills.

Differences between Mentors and Coaches
Mentors and speaking coaches are entirely different from one another. To know whether you should find a mentor, hire a coach, or even do both, we'll go over the differences between the two and how each can help you with your public speaking skills.

1. Mentors
2. Speaking Coaches
3. Using Both a Mentor and a Speaking Coach
4. How to Find a Mentor or Speaking Coach?

Mentors and Coaches

- **Mentors.** Mentoring is relationship-based. When you work with a mentor, you build a relationship with that person that is often long-term.
- **Speaking Coaches.** Coaches are task-based. If there is a particular area you are struggling with, they will focus on that area and help you to develop that particular skill.
- **Using Both a Mentor and a Speaking Coach.** Since mentors and coaches assist with different areas, your keynote speaking skills would likely end up more well-rounded. There is no rule book that says you cannot have both.
- **How to Find a Mentor or Coach?**
  - Networking events and social media sites.
  - First, decide what kind of speaker you want to be. Do you want to inspire? Make a million dollars? Do you want to shift the world?
  - Once you decide what kind of speaker you want to be, find out who is at the top in that field.
  - Attend the seminar of the speaker / workshop leader you want to emulate; usually they offer a training course— take it.

Step 10
Join a Speaker Association

There are many benefits to joining a speaker association if your passion truly lies in being a professional keynote speaker. Associations include groups like the National Speakers Association (NSA), the Women Speakers Association, and so many more globally. You can take your speaking career from the bottom to unimaginable levels.

There is also Toastmasters which is an entity in itself where you prepare and perform your own speeches weekly. In this chapter, you will learn how and why you should join a speaker association.

1. Why You Should Join a Speaker Association
2. Toastmasters – Honing Your Skills

Why You Should Join a Speaker Association

- Speaker associations are great educational, developmental, and networking resources for public speakers worldwide.
- They will provide you with learning tools such as; virtual learning courses that will assist you in honing your skills as well as building your brand and your business.
- Offer the opportunity to apply for speaking engagements and to be invited to speak at events.
- If you have little public speaking experience, consider the Academy Membership for the NSA. As you gain experience, you will be able to move up your membership level as you qualify for them.

Toastmasters – Honing Your Skills

- Each week you will learn by speaking in a supportive environment.
- As a bonus to learning to speak well in front of a crowd, you will learn how to be a confident and strong leader.

Step 11
Find Your Unique Voice

Every professional keynote speaker has their own unique voice. However, only a handful of those professional speakers let all of their unique voice show to their audience. Generally, this is because they haven't taken the time to find their unique voice and to hone it, so it stands out. This is a step that you don't want to skip because it could mean the difference between being a good keynote speaker and a great keynote speaker.

1. What is a Unique Voice?
2. How to Find Your Unique Voice

Find Your Voice

- **What is a Unique Voice?**
  - That sound you hear when you're giving a speech and you let all your reservations go.
  - If you want your audience to believe in what you're saying and to believe in you, you have to show them that *you* believe.
  - Why should they trust you? Why should they buy your product or follow your examples or do what you want them to do?

- **How to Find Your Unique Voice.** To find your voice, you need to think about the things that you truly care about.
  - What makes you cry/laugh?
  - If you were given a year to live, how would live it?
  - How would you want people to remember you?
  - What are your major regrets in life and what would you have done differently?
  - If you could meet one famous person, who would it be? Why? What would you talk to them about?
  - What are you most afraid of?

These questions and answers are the first step to helping you discover your unique voice.

Step 12
Take Off Your Impostor Mask

I'm not just a speaker. I am also a SoulBlazer; which is a Soul Life Coach. After working with thousands of clients over the past three decades, I realized that there are eight different personality types that appeared during life coaching sessions and the clients spoke from that perspective. I call these different personality types, the *Impostors*.

The Impostors are a cast of characters that star in the effective form of therapy called *SoulBlazing*. Impostors are a metaphor for the "masks" we wear every day and hide behind when confronted with something that we fear. They are also your EGO. *To take the Impostor quiz, visit, www.LisaHaisha.com*

They include:
1. The Wounded Inner child
2. Sex God(dess)
3. The Fixer
4. The Philosopher
5. The Counselor
6. The Clown
7. The Narcissist
8. The OverThinker

In order to be a great speaker, you need to know how to take off these masks.

Understand Your Impostor(s):

Once you have a strong understanding of which Impostor mask you wear, you can choose if it serves you or not. Here is how the Impostors reveal themselves negatively when speaking and in social situations:

- **The Wounded Inner child** comes across as the victim of life circumstances.
- **Sex God(dess)** usually has a magnetic charisma that they use to manipulate.
- **The Fixer** focuses on other people, so they don't have to look at their own faults.
- **The Philosopher** is often perceived as an elitist and a know-it-all.
- **The Counselor** helps other people, but sometimes has a hard time looking within.
- **The Clown** will do anything for a joke, even if it includes throwing someone under the bus.
- **The Narcissist** comes across as domineering, insensitive and aggressive.
- **The OverThinker** could overthink something to death, therefore never getting anything done.

Step 13
Create Evergreen Products

An evergreen product is a product that will have a long shelf life in the market. It's a product that will be able to be sold or distributed over and over again without going out-of-date or becoming irrelevant. Many keynote speakers use evergreen products to help market themselves and to bring in additional revenue. There are many different types of evergreen products that you can create even as a beginner keynote speaker.

1. eBooks
2. Videos
3. Email Series
4. Articles
5. Vlogs

What Are Evergreen Products

- **eBooks**. You can self-publish an eBook on Amazon or on your own website.
- **Videos.** Create a video series about your topic or niche, package it, and sell it as a set.
- **Email series.** To get subscribers to your email list, create an email series that contains evergreen content that your readers will find useful and informative. Later you can package that email series and sell it as an eBook.
- **Articles.** If you have a website or blog, write (or hire someone to write) evergreen articles for your website and social media sites.
- **Vlogs.** Videotaping yourself is sometimes more effective than the written word. When a client or fan experiences you speak in a video, they can connect to you in a unique way.

Your goal with these products is to share your knowledge with others in an effort to attract an audience, establish your expertise, and get booked as a speaker at various events. Keep these goals in mind.

Step 14
Establish Yourself as an Expert in Your Niche

Many people wonder if this means you need to have a college education. The answer is, *it depends*. If you want to talk about a medical phenomenon, then it would probably help your credibility to have a doctorate degree. Having a college degree isn't required to become a keynote speaker. However, you do need to have extensive knowledge about your topic.

1. Establishing Yourself as an Expert
2. Build Your Brand

How To Establish Yourself as an Expert

- Start a website or a blog where you post articles that fit within your topic, not necessarily all written by you.
- Invite other experts to guest post on your website.
- Attend as many conferences and events as possible that relate to your topic.

Build Your Brand

- Get social media, the more social media platforms you're active on, the better your chances are of getting noticed.
- Create digital content
  - Informational eBooks
  - Podcasts
  - Webinars
  - YouTube videos

The key to all of these methods is to provide valuable content. If you consistently provide valuable content, you will gain a following.

Step 15
Preparation Is Everything

When you are just starting out as a keynote speaker, it's important that you properly prepare your speech and yourself so that you are ready for your big moment on stage. The preparation process may seem tedious at first, but as you gain more experience, you will find that it will become second nature, and the whole process will get much easier. First, you will learn how to prepare your speech and then you will learn how to prepare to give your speech.

1. Preparing Your Speech
2. Preparing Yourself for Giving the Speech

Preparing Your Speech

- Choose Your Topic
- What is the Purpose of Your Speech?
- Find an Interesting Story
- Create an Outline
- Write the Speech

Preparing Yourself for Giving the Speech

- **Practice, Practice, Practice**. It can't be said enough, practicing your speech is a *must*. By reciting your speech out loud, you can hear how it sounds when it is being said.
- **Perfect Your Body Language.** Record yourself rehearsing your speech and using the movements and hand gestures to see how it all looks put together. Then you can decide what you need to add or take away to make it look more natural.
- **Visualize It.** Give yourself a pep talk beforehand, take some deep breaths, and go for it. You have what it takes to do this. Now go prove it to yourself.

You've finished. Before you go…

Tweet/share that you finished this book.

Please star rate this book.

Reviews are solid gold to writers. Please take a few minutes to give us some itty bitty feedback.

ABOUT THE AUTHOR

Lisa Haisha, M.A., is showing people how to "show up" in their own lives personally, professionally, and passionately with her fearless expression in all media as a globally sought-after life counselor and international speaker, Tedx speaker, and workshop facilitator. Lisa has been a guest on many news programs as a guest expert in communication, speaking, and as a life coach. She is also on the covers and regular contributor to many magazines over the past decade.

Lisa helps people discover the answers to these perennial soul-searching questions through SoulBlazing™, a process she created using her Impostor Model™. Her popular, decades-old, work has garnered the attention of Hollywood's elite, CEO's, and entrepreneurs, helping them deal with ego, fear and shame. This helped catapult their careers to a different level where they are both successful and *happy*.

Lisa's continued fascination with what makes people tick compelled her to travel for three decades to over 60 countries on seven continents. On this journey she compiled social and cultural research by studying the likes of the Sufis in Cappadocia, Shamans in Peru, Bedouins in Petra, and the Massai Tribes of Tanzania.

She took a five year journey interviewing orphans and compiled their answers to three magical questions in the book, *Whispers From Children's Hearts,* that started a global movement.

Look for her speaking events, seminars, and conferences in a city near you. Her upcoming books *SoulBlazing* and *Unmade Beds* will be released soon. Her TV show *SoulBlazing with Lisa Haisha,* where she interviews thought leaders, game changers and celebrities is available now on Amazon.

www.LisaHaisha.com
www.WhispersFromChildrensHearts.org

If you liked this Itty Bitty® Book you might also enjoy.

- **Your Amazing Itty Bitty® Prospects-to-Profits Lead Generation Book** – Erin Smilkstein

- **Your Amazing Itty Bitty® Self-Esteem Book** – Jade Elizabeth

- **Your Amazing Itty Bitty® Fear-Busting Book** – Lucetta Zaytoun

Or many of the many other Itty Bitty® books available on line.

www.ingramcontent.com/pod-product-compliance
Lightning Source LLC
Chambersburg PA
CBHW061304040426
42444CB00010B/2515